Flash cards

set 2

Musical Signs & Symbols

Essentials for Music Learning

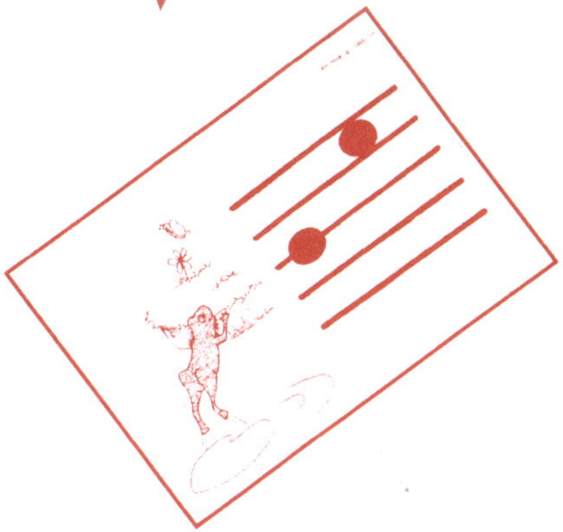

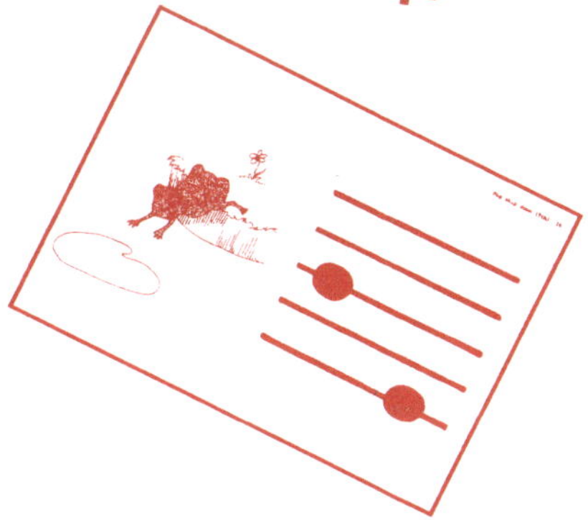

Helen Pace

Lee Roberts Music Publications, Inc.
Chatham, New York

Distributed By
HAL•LEONARD CORPORATION
7777 W. Bluemound Rd. P.O. Box 13819 Milwaukee, WI 53213

Musical Signs and Symbols Set 2

These unique flash cards introduce young students to the essential musical signs and symbols for developing musical literacy and understanding. Being able to recognize and deal effectively with these symbols is a basic aspect of musical thinking and the development of one's creative potential. Current research indicates that early musical experiences for children enhance their problem-solving capabilities in later life. These flash cards, used in musical game settings, will facilitate the development of each student's cognitive and creative skills.

While the cards are numbered in a sequence which moves from the most basic to more complex concepts, they actually can be used in an endless variety of sequences to allow for the many different learning situations. An example of this flexibility can be seen in how one would help the student recognize the very basic concept of whether the second tone of a melodic pattern *moves up, down or stays on the same pitch.* Teacher or parent could play two notes as the child finds and holds up the appropriate card. Or, one could hold up the card and let the child play with their pointer finger the appropriate two-note sequence. Extending this further after treble and bass clefs have been introduced, students could either find their two-note sequence *high or low* on the keyboard, or respond with the appropriate card. Still later, the two- and three-note patterns in the set can be mixed together to be found either high, middle or low on the keyboard.

In Set 1, basic beat and relative duration are introduced, then continued with more complex patterns in Set 2. Eventually, the two sets of cards should be merged to provide a rich source of melodic patterns, intervals and basic rhythms to be applied regularly during lessons.

In the initial stages, the little character figures on one side of the card help students visualize the basic concepts being presented. On the reverse side, however, the symbol or pattern appears without the character figures. Students should be encouraged to work from this side of the card as soon as possible, relying on the reverse side mainly as a check.

Using the cards for a few minutes as a regular part of daily practice, plus short review drills during each lesson with the teacher, will ensure that all students develop the rudimentary knowledge for a lifetime of enjoyable musical participation.

2381

Quar-ter, quar-ter, quar-ter, half-note-dot 2

Whole note (Whole-note-hold-it)   3

Quar-ter, quar-ter, quar-ter, quar-ter, whole-note-hold-it 4

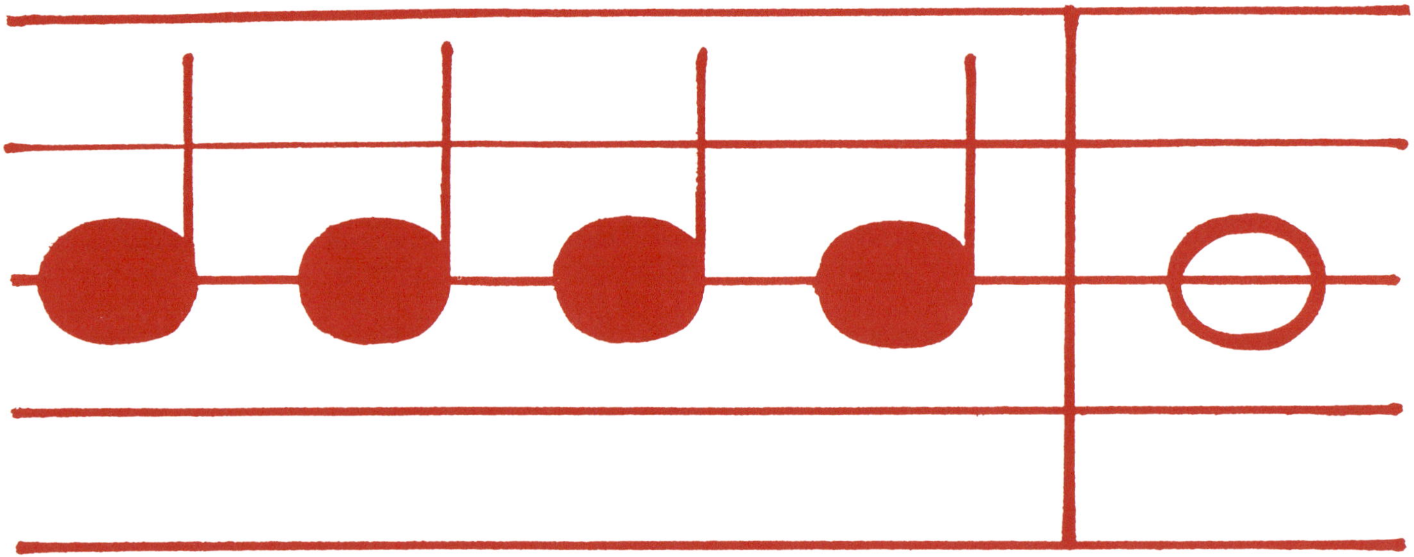

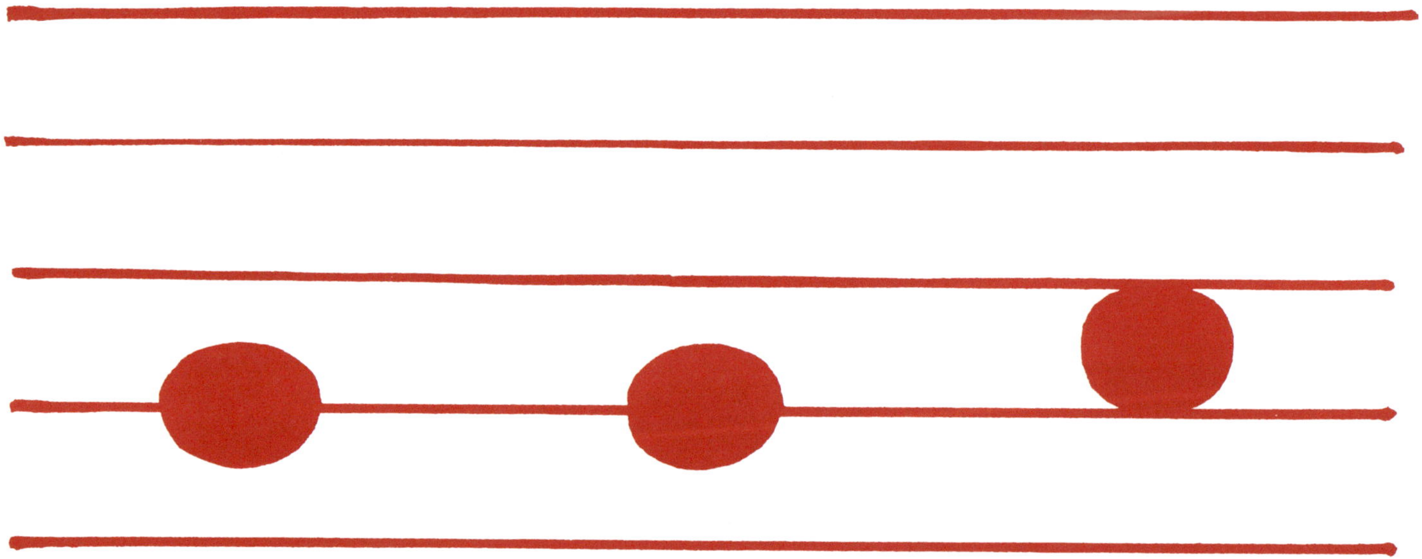

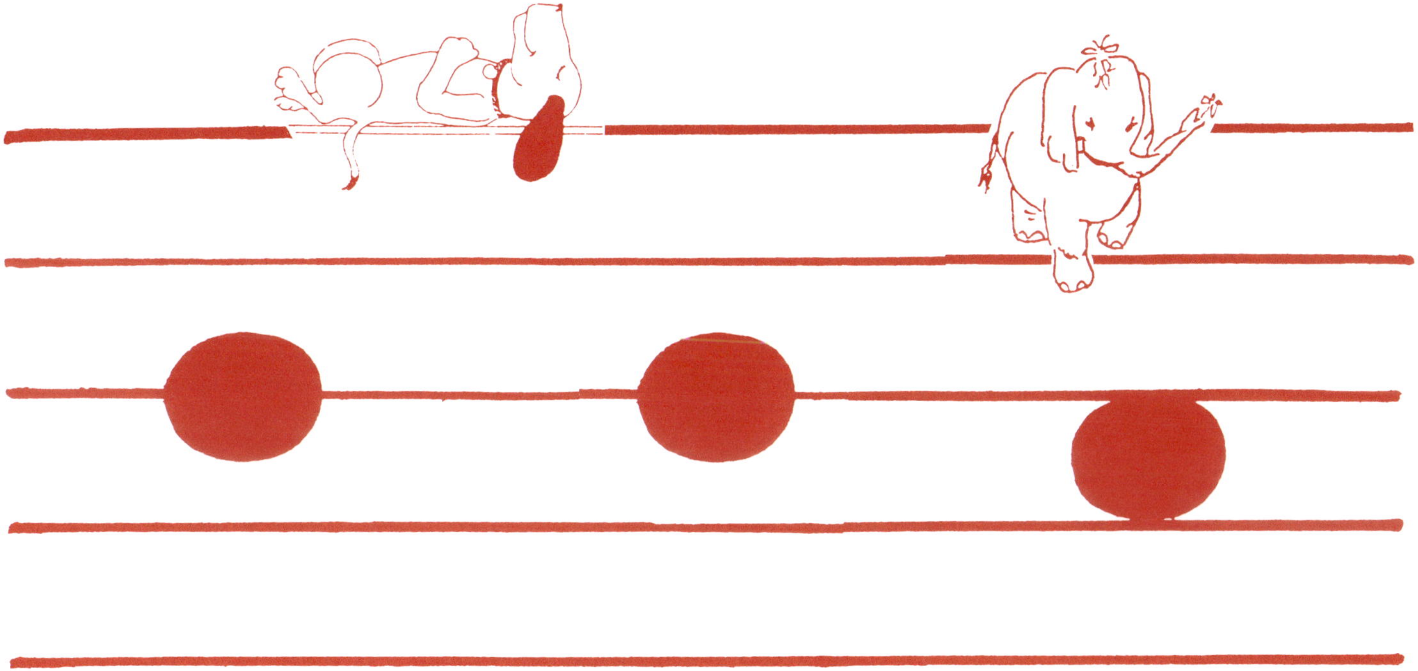

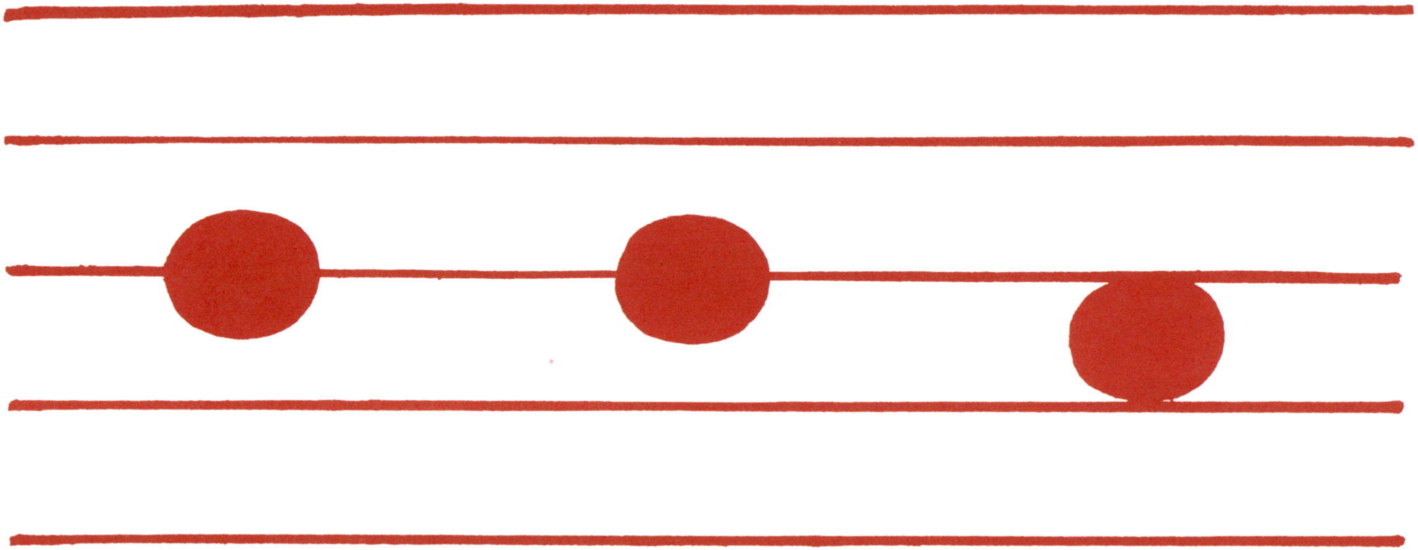

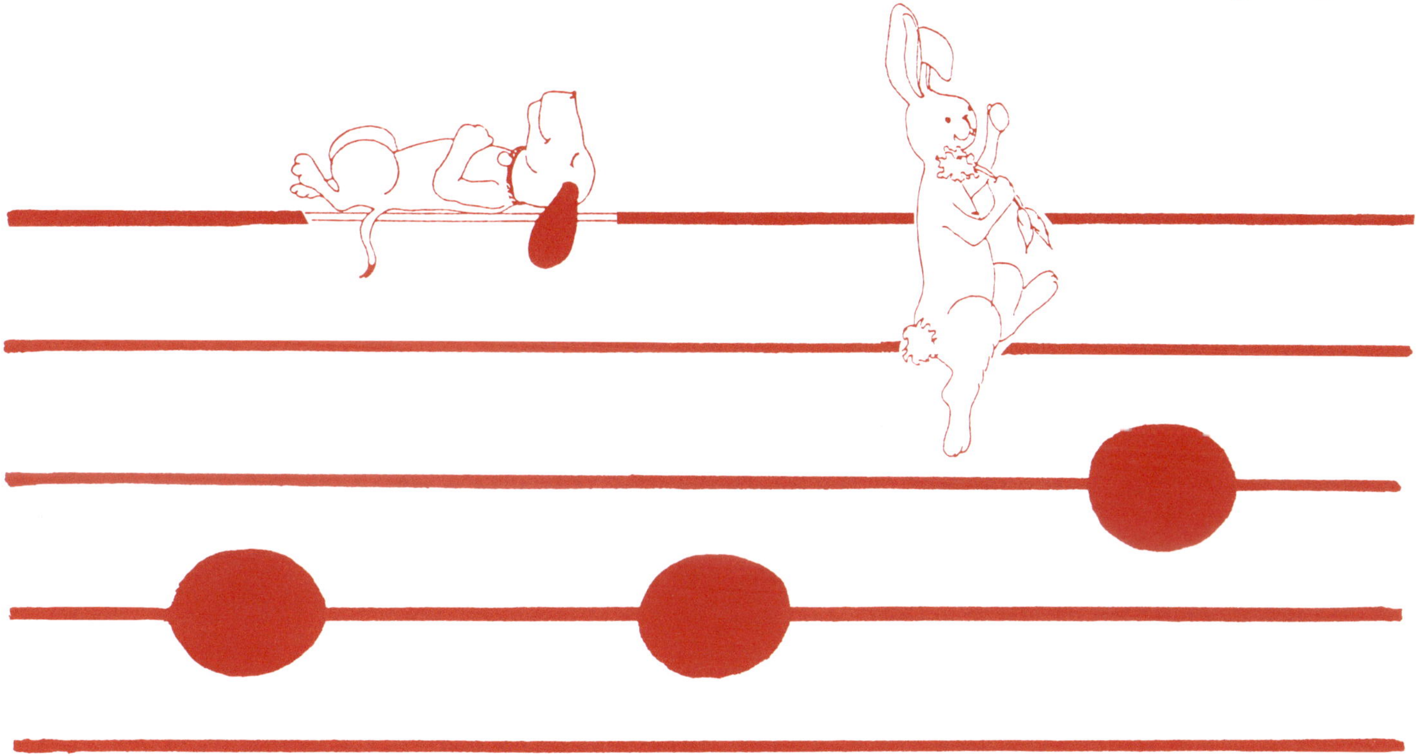

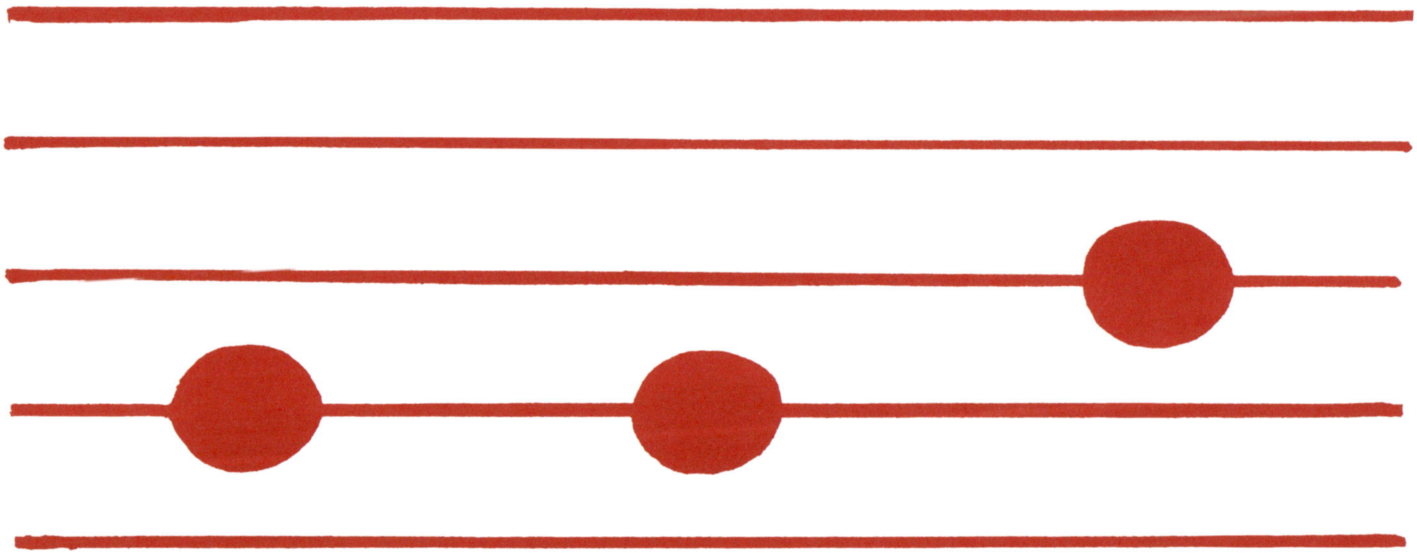

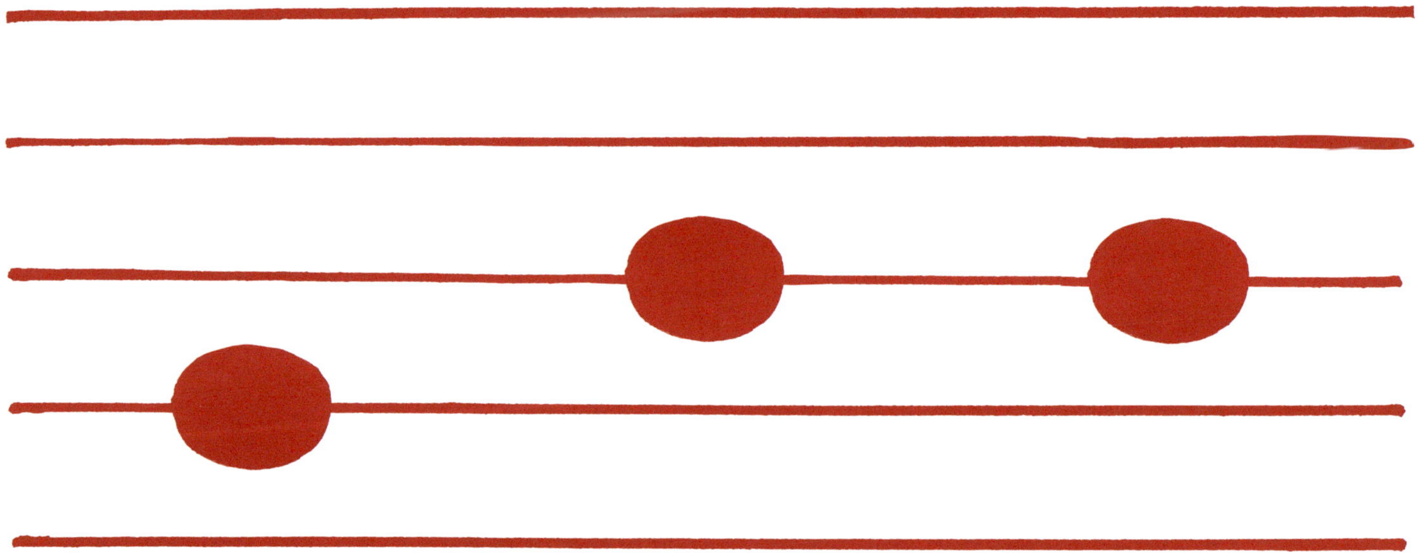

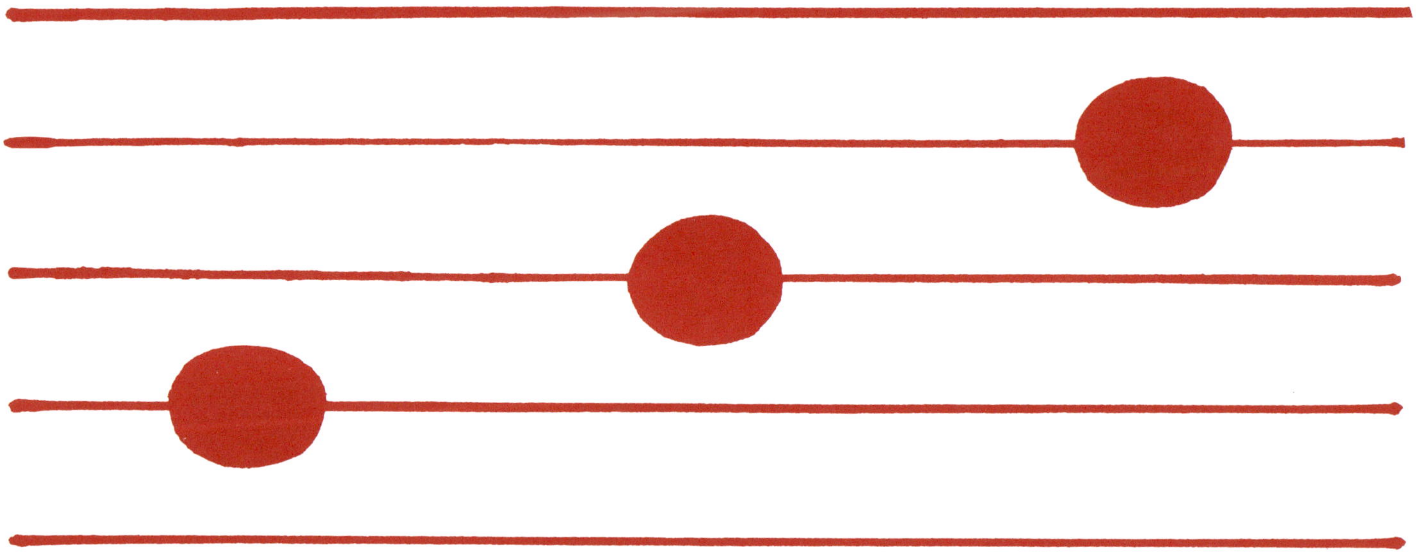

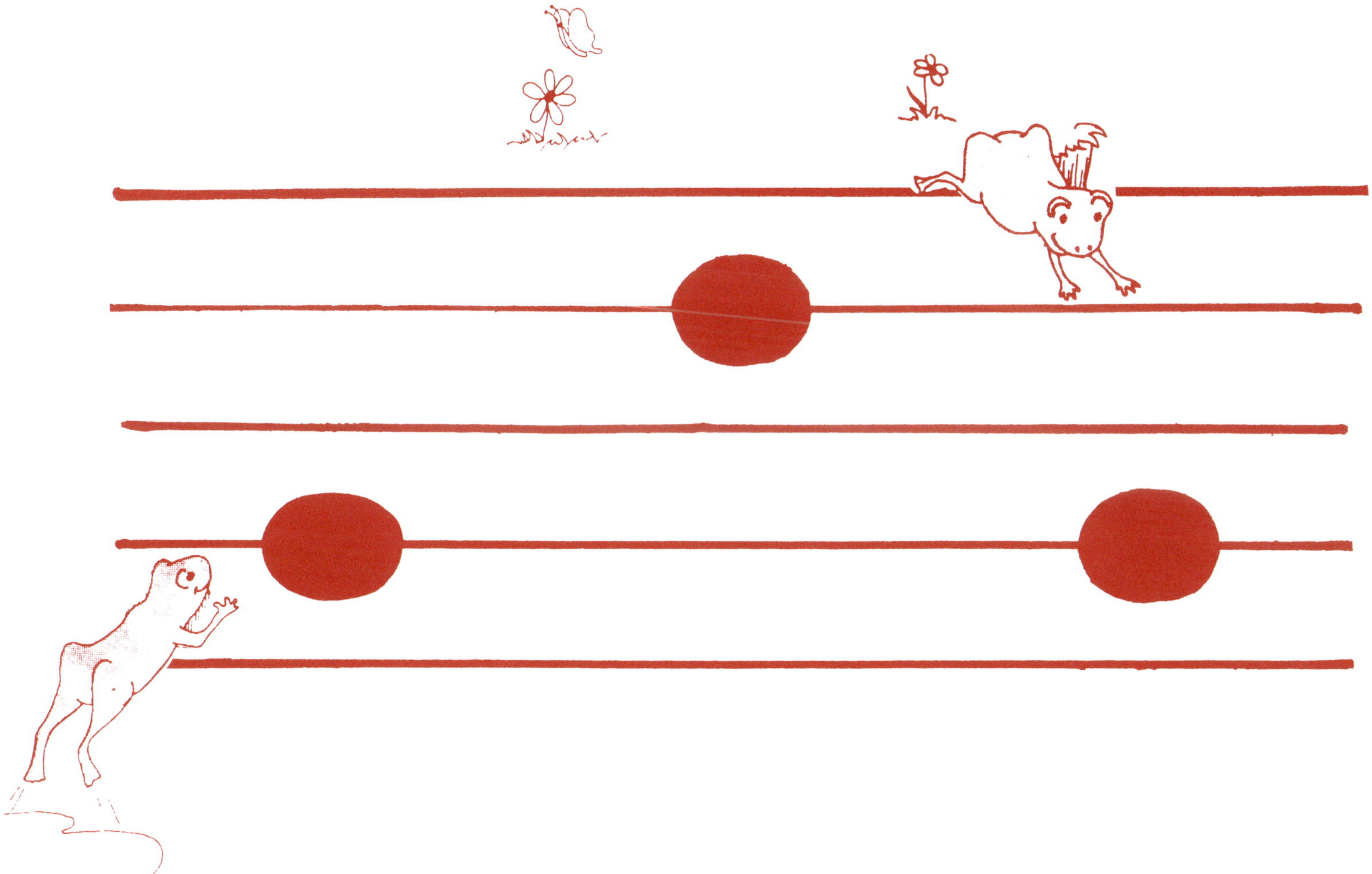

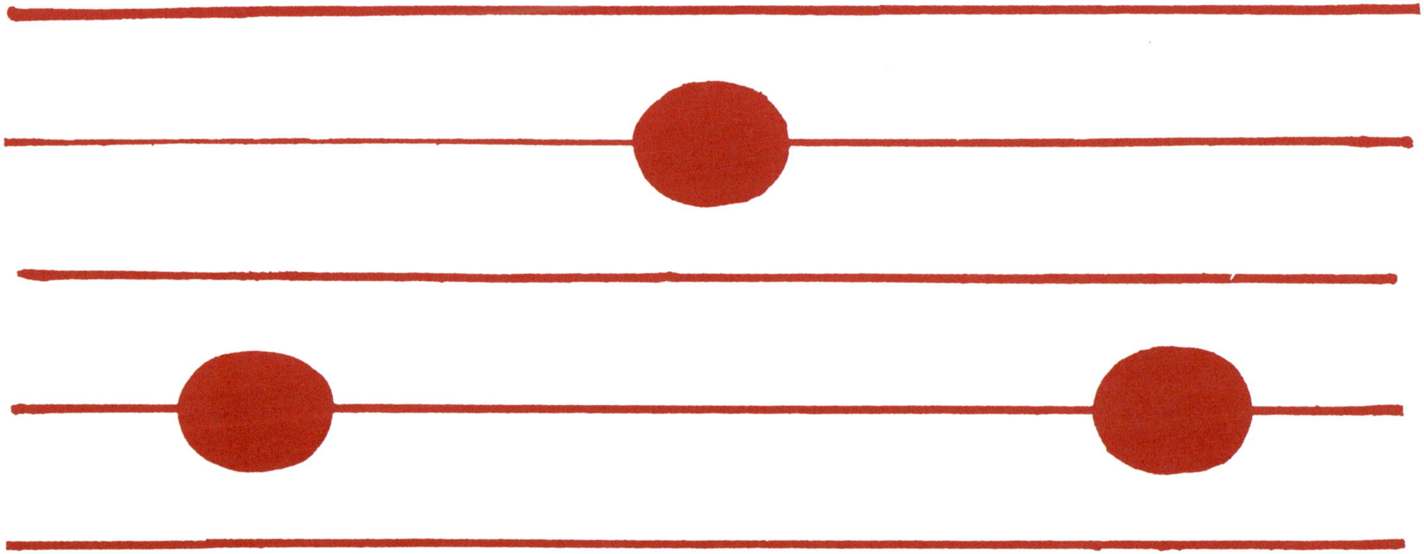

U.S. $6.95
ISBN 0-7935-9518-6
0 73999 74780 5
HL00372381